For
a daddy and his boys

*Father, make us one*
*in Christ forever.*

New Growth Press, Greensboro, NC 27404
Copyright © 2018 by Irene Sun

Cover/Interior Illustrations: Alex Foster, alex-foster.com
Cover/Interior Layout: Trish Mahoney, themahoney.com

ISBN 978-1-945270-79-6 (Print)
ISBN 978-1-945270-74-1 (eBook)

Library of Congress Cataloging-in-Publication Data
Names: Sun, Irene, 1981- author.
Title: God counts : numbers in his word and his world / Irene Sun.
Description: Greensboro : New Growth Press, 2018.
Identifiers: LCCN 2018043747 (print) | LCCN 2018046376 (ebook) | ISBN
  9781945270741 (ebook) | ISBN 9781945270796 (trade cloth)
Subjects:  LCSH: Numbers in the Bible--Juvenile literature.
Classification: LCC BS680.N8 (ebook) | LCC BS680.N8 S86 2018 (print) | DDC
  242/.62--dc23
LC record available at https://lccn.loc.gov/2018043747

Printed in Malaysia

26 25 24 23 22 21 20 19          2 3 4 5 6

# GOD COUNTS

## NUMBERS IN HIS WORD AND HIS WORLD

IRENE SUN

In the beginning,
God created numbers.
Numbers declare the glory of God.

**One** tells us that God is the first and best.

The Lord, he is God.
There is no other.
God is the **one** and only,
the only **one**.

DEUTERONOMY 6:4

**2** Two tells us
we are not alone.

In the beginning,
God made **two** people,
Adam and Eve.
They walked with God, side by side.
They talked to God, face to face.

Adam and Eve were
not like the animals.
They looked a lot like each other,
but also a little bit different.
Most of all, they looked like God.

GENESIS 2:27

**Three** tells us God is love.

God the Father,

God the Son,

**God the Holy Spirit.**

**Three** in one, one in **three**,
They love one another,
like a family.

3

**Three** tells us that God loves us.
Jesus died in our place
on the cross at **three** o'clock.
Jesus rose again on the **third** day to
make us a part of his family.

MATTHEW 27:46; 1 CORINTHIANS 15:4

**Four** tells us God made everything beautiful.

God made **four** rivers in the Garden of Eden and **four** wings on every butterfly.

GENESIS 2:10

There are **four** creatures before God's throne, singing: "Holy, holy, holy is the Lord God Almighty!"

REVELATION 4:7-8

# 5

## Five tells us God speaks.

God's Word is sweet like honey.
Moses wrote **five** books of the Bible
to tell people about God.

PSALM 19:10

God tells his children,
"I love you."
God tells his children,
"Love me by listening to what I say."
God speaks to his children
because he loves them.

DEUTERONOMY 6:4-5; JOHN 14:15

Six tells us God hates sin.

Here are **six** things that the Lord hates,

unkind eyes,

a lying tongue,

hands that hurt,

a wicked heart,

disobedient feet,

and lies that separate people.

PROVERBS 6:16-19

**7**

## **Seven** tells us God is with us.

The Lord said to Joshua,
"Be strong and courageous, because I am with you.
March around Jericho for **seven** days.
Bring **seven** priests with **seven** horns.

On the **seventh** day,
march around the city **seven** times."
Joshua obeyed, and the walls of Jericho
came tumbling down.

JOSHUA 1:9; 6:4

**Eight** tells us God rescues his children

God said to Noah,
"Build an ark. Bring the animals. Bring your family."
Noah obeyed.

The sky rained and rained, week after week,
Until water covered the earth.
God rescued **eight** people in the ark.

GENESIS 8:1, 16

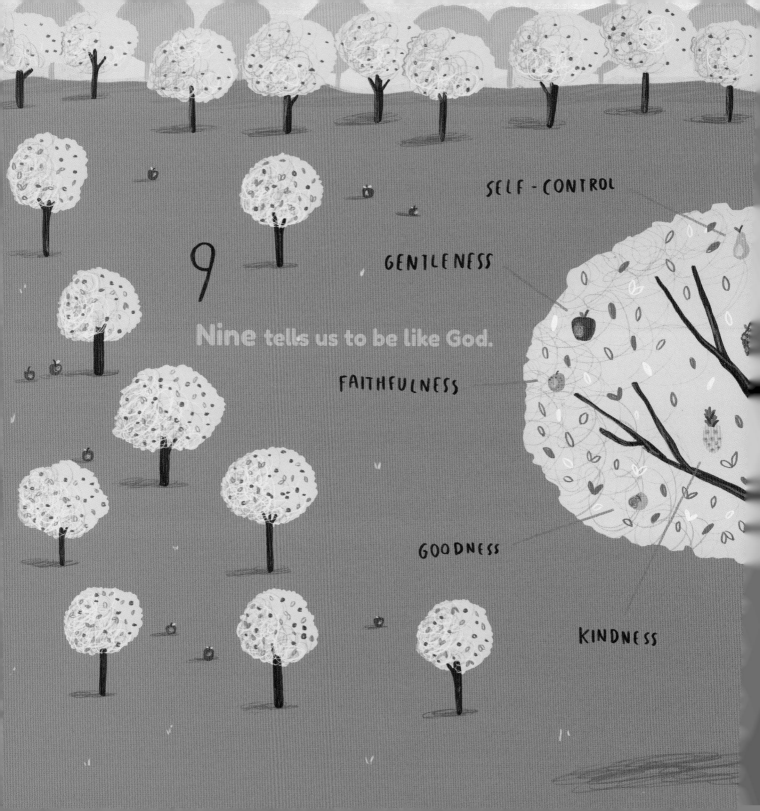

9

Nine tells us to be like God.

SELF-CONTROL

GENTLENESS

FAITHFULNESS

GOODNESS

KINDNESS

LOVE

JOY

PEACE

PATIENCE

Apple trees bear apples.
Banana trees bear bananas.
The Holy Spirit helps God's children to be like Jesus.
Jesus is full of love, joy, peace, patience, kindness,
goodness, faithfulness, gentleness, and self-control.

God wants his children to be like him.

GALATIANS 5:22-23; 1 PETER 1:16

**Ten tells us God does not want any of his children to be lost.**

Once, there was a lady who had **ten** coins.
She loved her coins, and she loved counting them.
1, 2, 3, 4, 5, 6, 7, 8, 9, 10.

One day, she lost one coin.
She looked here. No coin.
She looked there. No coin.

Finally, she found her coin!
She was so happy.

God seeks after his lost children.
God is happy when he finds them!

LUKE 15:8-10; 2 PETER 3:9

11

**Eleven** tells us God forgives us.

Jesus chose twelve people to be his disciples.
Jesus loved all of them.
He washed their feet.
He gave them bread.
But Judas did not love Jesus,
So Judas ran away.
He did not come back.

JOHN 13:21, 30

The other **eleven** disciples also left Jesus.
But the **eleven** disciples came back.
They were all sorry,
And Jesus forgave them.

MATTHEW 26:56; 75

Twelve tells us we will live with God forever.

12

One day, God will take us to his home.
There will be no more pain, no more crying.
There will be the tree of life with **twelve** kinds of fruit.
There will be **twelve** shiny gates.
There will be no sun, because the Lord will be our light.

REVELATION 21:12; 22:2

**Infinity** is a symbol for something that has no end.

God is **infinite**.
He is beyond numbers, beyond time, beyond space.
He is the Almighty,
who was and is and is to come.

REVELATION 4:8

Jesus is **infinite**.
But Jesus did not think about his greatness.
He became a baby in Mary's womb,
a small and narrow place for the maker of stars.

PHILIPPIANS 2:5-8

**God Counts.**

God counts every fish in the sea,
every star in the sky.
God counts every hair on your head,
every tear you cry.

God counts all of your steps
Until you walk with him side by side.

1
2
3
4
5
6
7
8
9
10
11
12

God counts all of your days
Until you see him face to face.
God created numbers to declare his glory.